# FIGHT F(

# FREED(

A young woman's quest to raise awareness about
Anorexia Nervosa.

## Rose Anne Evans

## 1

# Testimonials

"I really like how the book is organised and the way it directly addresses different groups. I feel like it should be in every school, CAMHS outpatients, etc."

"It is beautiful, positive, easy to read and helpful."

"I love reading your work. It really helps to get an understanding of such issues and I really wish more people had the chance to get an insight like this."

ISBN: 9781521457719
This book is also available in coloured print.
This book is also available in E-Book form.

Despite the endless hours of my childhood spent playing doctors and nurses, I don't claim to be a health or medical professional, but have merely used my own experiences of living with an eating disorder to explain how it made me feel, as well as what has and hasn't helped me on my journey to recovery.

Please talk to those around you, including clinicians, to help you to get the best help and advice for your individual case.

# Dedications

In loving Memory of:

My Grandad, Ronald Evans, who was always there for me,
especially during my time in hospital.

This book is also dedicated to:

My parents, Alan and Jacqueline Evans, because without their
continued support, I wouldn't be where I am today.

My sister Georgie Evans, who has been so mature and supportive
throughout my illness.

My best friend, Alice Hiley, who has helped me get through all of
the difficult times.

My church family who have supported me from the beginning.

All of the staff at The Priory Hospital, Cheadle Royal, whose
amazing help has allowed me to live again.

The professionals who have been part of my care and who have
helped me to come this far.

# About the author

Originally from Halifax, West Yorkshire, Rose Anne Evans (20) now lives in York, where she is studying French and German at university.

As a Young Champion for the mental health charity 'Time To Change', she is dedicated to raising awareness and understanding of mental illness and, in particular, eating disorders.

This is the first book that Rose Anne has written and she hopes it helps sufferers, family and professionals to gain more of an understanding of what Anorexia Nervosa is and how best to fight it.

For more information, or to find out more, please visit roseanneevans.com

# About this Book

Rose Anne aims to help people to develop a better understanding of what eating disorders actually are, as well as what it feels like to live with one.

Her book contains extracts from her journal as well as poetry she has written and it specifically concentrates on Anorexia Nervosa, as this is the condition she has personally experienced. It is packed full of memoirs and advice for sufferers, carers/supporters, professionals and members of the public.

# Anorexia portrayed in the media

Every week, there is always a story in the newspaper, or a picture posted on social media of a person with an eating disorder (and more often than not, Anorexia Nervosa). Many of these publications include a 'before' and 'after' photo of the sufferer in order to draw attention to the article. However, such pieces can be triggering for those suffering from an eating disorder and may make them feel like they are 'not thin enough'.

My aim is not to create a book full of triggering information or photos, but instead to create a 'safe space', where people can relate to certain experiences, rather than be triggered by them.

# Contents

FIGHT FOR FREEDOM ...........................................................................1

TESTIMONIALS ....................................................................................2

DEDICATIONS .....................................................................................4

ABOUT THE AUTHOR ............................................................................5
ABOUT THIS BOOK ..............................................................................6
ANOREXIA PORTRAYED IN THE MEDIA........................................................6

CONTENTS.........................................................................................7

FOREWORD .....................................................................................10

THE FACTS ABOUT ANOREXIA NERVOSA.................................................11

WHAT IS ANOREXIA NERVOSA? ............................................................12
BEHAVIOURAL SIGNS .........................................................................13
PHYSICAL SIGNS................................................................................15
THE MYTHS AND FACTS ABOUT ANOREXIA ...............................................16
MY EXPERIENCE OF CO-MORBIDITY (OTHER CONDITIONS RELATED TO ANOREXIA) ...18
WHAT DOES IT FEEL LIKE TO LIVE WITH AN EATING DISORDER? ....................21

MY DIARY ........................................................................................24

THE THREE-WAY FIGHT.......................................................................25
GETTING A BOOST .............................................................................27
NEW YEAR'S RESOLUTION ...................................................................28
SQUASH .........................................................................................29
REMEMBER HOW ANOREXIA MAKES YOU FEEL: .........................................30
ROSE ANNE'S PAGE OF POSITIVITY ........................................................31
I WANT TO BE 'NORMAL' .....................................................................32

HOLIDAY OF A LIFETIME............................................................33

KEEP FIGHTING ....................................................................34

I AM BEGINNING TO FEEL 'NORMAL' AGAIN ..............................35

MOVING AWAY FROM MY MEAL PLAN .....................................36

REALISATION ABOUT HUNGER.................................................37

CHRISTMAS DAY...................................................................38

BOXING DAY .......................................................................40

FEELING TRAPPED ...............................................................41

FIGHT FOR YOUR LIFE ...........................................................42

MEASURING MY ACHIEVEMENTS .............................................43

DISTORTED IMAGE ...............................................................44

WISDOM FOR WARRIORS........................................................46

THERAPY ...........................................................................47

LETTER OF ENCOURAGEMENT DURING DIFFICULT TIMES ...............53

DISTRESS TOLERANCE ...........................................................55

MINDFULNESS .....................................................................66

LIVING FOR YOUR VALUES .....................................................70

TAKING THE LEAP ................................................................72

DEAR BODY OF MINE............................................................74

YOUR BODY IS YOUR FRIEND..................................................76

HELPING YOUR LOVED ONE.....................................................78

SUPPORTING A FRIEND..........................................................79

THE IMPORTANCE OF FRIENDSHIP ...........................................80

FRIEND Q & A .....................................................................85

MY ADVICE FOR FRIENDS.......................................................87

OPENING UP TO MY PARENTS .................................................88

INTERVIEW: A MOTHER'S PERSPECTIVE .....................................90

FAMILY THERAPY.................................................................92

MY ADVICE FOR PARENTS ......................................................93

## PROFESSIONALS .................................................................. 94

EATING DISORDERS IN SCHOOLS ................................................ 95
GP'S ..................................................................................... 97
MY ADVICE FOR GP'S .............................................................. 98
MY EXPERIENCE OF DIFFERENT THERAPIES ................................. 99
TIPS FOR CLINICIANS ............................................................. 103
TIPS FOR DIETICIANS ............................................................. 105
USEFUL AIDS ........................................................................ 108
EATING DISORDER RESEARCH AT THE UNIVERSITY OF YORK ........... 109

## BIRD FLYING FREE ............................................................ 111

BE A FRIEND TO YOURSELF ..................................................... 112
REACHING RECOVERY GOALS .................................................. 115
MUSIC IN RECOVERY ............................................................. 117

## POETRY ......................................................................... 119

A LIFE WITHOUT ANA ............................................................ 120
MY JOURNEY TO RECOVERY .................................................... 121
SO CALLED FRIEND ............................................................... 122
MAKE A WISH UPON A STAR .................................................... 125
FIGHTER ............................................................................. 126
I WANT TO BE FREE ............................................................... 128
THE DREAM I'VE LONGED TO CHASE ........................................ 130

## THANK YOU ..................................................................... 131

# Foreword

*Contributed by BABCP-accredited Cognitive Behavioural Therapist Dan Round, whose therapy has been an invaluable part of my recovery from Anorexia.*

It has been my pleasure to have met Rose Anne along her journey to recovery and to walk with her on that unknown path that many have embarked upon and others have yet to begin. The road to recovery starts with the first step, but can be a frightening terrain to navigate.

Rose Anne's story holds hope, her book a guide. Passionate to help others, Rose Anne is a Time to Change Young Champion and has also run events in aid of the eating disorder charity Beat. Wherever you are, whoever you are, Rose Anne's book will be an inspiration to those brave people who face recovery and all who accompany them.

Rose Anne is a remarkable young lady who has found her way from the difficulties of having an eating disorder, to understanding herself as a person who has autism. She is creative and compassionate, kind and thoughtful.

She loves playing squash and has an amazing talent of learning languages quickly. She is currently a student at the University of York, where she is reading a BA in French and German.

# The Facts About
# Anorexia Nervosa

# What is Anorexia Nervosa?

According to the UK's eating disorder charity BEAT, Anorexia is a serious mental illness where people keep their body weight low by dieting, vomiting, using laxatives or excessively exercising. The way people with anorexia see themselves is often at odds with how they are seen by others and they will usually challenge the idea that they should gain weight. For example, they often have a distorted image of themselves, thinking that they're fat when they're not. People affected by anorexia often go to great attempts to hide their behaviour from family and friends.

# Behavioural signs

★ Fear of being fat

★ Being preoccupied with body weight

★ Having a distorted perception of their body weight or shape

★ Not realising the seriousness of their problem

★ Being dishonest about what they have eaten

★ Constantly thinking about food

★ Following a strict diet

★ Counting the calories in food

★ Avoiding foods they perceive as 'scary'

★ Skipping meals

★ Not eating around other people

★ Hiding food

★ Taking slimming or diet pills

★ Being rigid

★ Exercising excessively

★ Obsessive behaviour

★ Vomiting

★ Misusing laxatives

★ Isolating themselves from social situations

# Physical signs

★ Severe weight loss

★ Females may have irregular or no periods

★ Having sleeping difficulties

★ Tiredness

★ Dizziness

★ Having stomach pains

★ Being constipated or bloated

★ Feeling cold

★ Growth of soft, fine hair on their body (Lanugo)

★ Hair loss

★ Irritability

★ Moodiness

★ Having concentration difficulties

★ Weakness

★ Losing muscle strength

★ Having low blood pressure

**15**

# The myths and facts about anorexia

*Anorexia is a very complicated illness and therefore it is often misunderstood by the general public. Here are just a few of the common misconceptions surrounding Anorexia.*

**Myth**: Only teenage girls can develop Anorexia Nervosa

**Fact**: Both males and females of all ages and cultural backgrounds can develop anorexia.

**Myth**: Once your weight is restored, you no longer have an eating disorder.

**Fact**: Anorexia Nervosa is a mental illness and although weight restoration helps to improve cognitive processing, it can take a long time for a person to fully recover from an eating disorder.

**Myth**: People with anorexia are just 'attention-seekers'.

**Fact**: Anorexia Nervosa is a serious illness and in fact for many sufferers, anorexia may try to hide any evidence of its existence to the world.

**Myth**: Anorexia is a 'glamourous illness'.

**Fact**: Although it is sometimes portrayed this way in the media, anorexia is definitely not a glamourous illness. There is certainly no

**16**

fun in being constantly cold, tired, feeling weak and dizzy and not being able to function in everyday life.

**Myth**: Anorexia is just about food and weight.

**Fact**: Having a preoccupation with food and body weight is a symptom of Anorexia, but the illness is much more complicated. Since this is a mental illness, there is generally an underlying problem which also needs to be addressed.

**Myth**: People with Anorexia don't eat anything.

**Fact**: Our bodies need a certain amount of energy each day in order to create a balance with the amount of energy it uses for essential processes such as respiration. For people with Anorexia, their energy intake is less than their energy output, but that does not mean that they don't eat anything.

# My experience of co-morbidity (other conditions related to Anorexia)

## OCD

From a very young age, I have experienced what I now know to be intrusive thoughts. These always seemed to relate to those closest to me somehow being hurt. For example, I used to insist on planning fire escape routes in the house in order to ensure that my family would be able to safely evacuate the building. Because I can't remember a time when these thoughts didn't exist, I just assumed that everyone experienced this and never talked about it. It wasn't until the age of around 14 after having a conversation with a friend, that I realised others didn't think in the same way.

OCD affected me more internally than externally and so, to the world, nothing seemed different. Inside, however, it was a totally different story. I spent many days wrapped up in my own thoughts, thinking 'if I don't do [x], then something bad will happen.

In a similar way to Anorexia, these intrusive thoughts do regularly pop into my mind, but the difference now is the meaning I attach to them. Whereas before, I would have become really anxious about why I was even thinking that thought in the first place and then translate this to mean 'I am a bad person'', nowadays I am able to have the thought, realise it's 'just a thought', and allow it to fade away. I have learnt that not judging my thoughts or myself is the best way to fight against my OCD.

## Autism/Asperger's Syndrome

Since being diagnosed with autism, I have been able to make sense of so many things, especially those relating to my eating disorder. For example, many situations involving food, including dining rooms or restaurants are very 'fast' and 'busy' environments. But, unbeknown to me, I would often experience sensory overload because I was unable to cope with all of the stimulation around me. This led to being stuck in situations such as choosing a meal in a restaurant or choosing what to buy in the supermarket.

Subconsciously, I needed a way to cope with this problem and so for me, choosing food based on its calorie content was much less stressful and allowed me to get out of the situation much quicker. Being aware of this has made all the difference, as I am now much more able to either pre-empt when I might have a sensory overload, or at least know how to calm myself down.

For me, having autism also means that I find it difficult to make decisions, because I am not able to 'tune in' to my feelings in order to know what I want/need. This was another reason that I began calorie counting because I could make a choice more easily, without getting frustrated at myself for taking too long.

I know that Autism isn't something that has a 'cure', but that isn't necessarily a bad thing. As with everything, you can't have negatives without at least a few positives. For me, empathy isn't something I lack, but rather something I have lots of. I sometimes explain it as being over sensitive to other people's emotions. However, this is a trait that I really value, because it often allows me to help other people. After talking about this in therapy, I am now more able to use this hypersensitivity in a positive way by knowing the

**19**

boundaries between being empathetic and getting too involved with other people's problems.

For anyone who has autism, my biggest piece of advice would be to embrace it. Although it can be very frustrating at times, you wouldn't be you without autism and the likelihood is, it's made you a stronger person. Once you learn to accept yourself and be confident with who you are, other people are also more likely to accept you.

# What does it feel like to live with an eating disorder?

*Trying to explain what Anorexia feels like is not easy, but I feel it is important for someone to be able to 'see into the mind' of anorexia. Here is my experience of how it felt to be constantly fighting an eating disorder.*

To begin with, Anorexia was like a friend to me. It helped me to cope whenever I was feeling out of control or stressed. Controlling what and when I ate gave me structure and a routine, which is something I have always felt the need to have.
But the positivity ends there.

So what's anorexia really like?

I felt as if I was a puppet and Anorexia was holding the strings. It had complete control over me and, what's more, it left me feeling lonely, isolated and frustrated. Deep down, I really did want to recover and have a more normal life, but the anorexic voice inside my head was telling me that I wasn't good enough and that I wouldn't be able to cope without it. This, along with fear of the unknown meant that recovery became a risk. I didn't know if I would cope with difficult situations without Anorexia and so at the time, I didn't see the point in taking that chance.

However, there were so many negative aspects of my illness that I seemed to ignore.

The cold constantly biting me, even when it is "shorts and T-shirt" weather for everyone else.

**21**

Going to sleep every night not knowing if I would wake up the next morning.

Having a panic attack at the sight or even the thought of food.

A constant mind-battle between me and Anorexia during mealtimes.

After being admitted to a specialist eating disorder inpatient unit, I realised that I couldn't live the rest of my life being controlled by anorexia. So as difficult as it was, I began to take small steps towards recovery. The thing about recovery is that it isn't straight forward and, since it involves facing your fear several times a day, it can often be very anxiety-provoking.

I knew that I needed to keep on fighting and not listen to anorexia, but this was often easier said than done. It did still feel like my eating disorder was a safety net and, without it, I would have to face the unknown.

A few times, I stumbled at a certain hurdle where, as soon as I reached my "target weight", I found myself resorting back to restricting to ensure my weight didn't go any higher. But on the way back up from my last relapse, I allowed my body to decide what weight it wanted to be.

I exceeded the target set for me in hospital and then my weight went higher than it had ever been before. At first, I found this very difficult, but then I remembered that I am no longer a teenager and my adult body has never actually been given the chance to reach its preferred weight. And once I allowed this to happen, I started to see how positive recovery could be.

**22**

For me, restoring weight also meant restoring my personality and it brought back the cheerful, bouncy and loving person who had disappeared for a few years. But my experience also allowed me to build strength and resilience. The years of therapy not only helped me to deal with my illness, but also with the stresses of everyday life.

I'm so glad I decided to choose recovery when I did, because now I can enjoy life and take the lead role in my own life with only the occasional guest appearance from anorexia.

**23**

# MY DIARY

Sharing parts of your diary with the world is scary, right?

True.

But to me, nothing is scarier than being controlled by an illness which robs you of your life. And if sharing my story can make just one person's journey to recovery slightly less daunting, it's *totally* worth it!

In this section, I have chosen what I think are the most significant diary entries since my fight began. There were times of despair, fear, hope, love and every emotion in between, but I tried my best to stay positive throughout and I hope this is apparent in my diary entries.

# The three-way fight

*A diary entry from 10.08.15*
*This entry depicts my sudden realisation that I had more than one battle to fight (and win).*

It was the dreaded Monday morning weigh-in today and I hardly slept last night.

My weight went up quite a lot this week, which I struggled with, especially seeing as I was so tired. I don't understand my head sometimes though! Last week I was upset because my weight stayed the same and this week I'm upset because my weight went up! I really can't win! On the other hand I had a really helpful therapy session, in which I realised that I am trying to fight three different things in my head all at once.

Firstly, there's Demon (AKA Anorexia). He makes me feel guilty about eating which leads me to ruminate constantly.

Then there's Perfect Peter (AKA Perfectionism) who insists on everything being 100% correct 100% of the time.

Obviously, that is impossible and so I just end up feeling inadequate.

Finally, there's OCD, who often seems to work alongside Perfect Peter and Demon, but then sometimes works against them.

Once I manage to get one under control, another will become stronger and so it feels like I'm stuck in a cycle of four different people in my head all trying to fight for the role as 'driver'.

## 25

DEMON

'Don't listen to anyone else - they are lying to you'

'I will make you into a stronger person'

'You don't need help'

'You're not worth it'

'Nobody likes you'

'I can make you perfect'

'Don't eat'

'You're a bad person'

'Physical pain is better than mental pain'

'You're weak'

'Listen to me and you will be happy'

'I'm your one and only friend'

'Other people suffer and so should you'

'You don't deserve to eat'

'I can give you the control you don't have'

'Just a little bit thinner'

'I will help you to take away all of your worries and troubles'

'You're not ill enough'

PETER

'You need 100% every time'

'You're a failure'

'You need to make a perfect recovery'

'You're going to let everyone down.'

'You're not good enough'

'You're not worthy'

'You have to do better'

'Everyone else is better than you'

'If something isn't perfect, you have to do it again.'

'You need to be a perfect friend'

'Nobody will like you if you're not perfect'

'You need a perfect mind body and personality.'

# Getting a boost

*A diary entry from 17.08.15*
*On days like this, having such a wonderful best friend just instantly lifted up my spirits.*

The day didn't start out very well but tonight, I'm feeling great! I put on a lot of weight this week, which I found hard to cope with. As well as this, I found out today that my therapist is leaving.

It's going to be really difficult to see her go because she really understands me and she is the only person who I feel comfortable fully opening up to. Hopefully though, I will feel at ease with the new therapist too and so I will try my hardest to make the most out of it.

Despite this, I had a lovely surprise tonight! I have been feeling down and panicky all day, but a skype call from my best friend Alice has given me an almighty boost! It was so lovely to see her and I'm happy to hear she's enjoying uni! I honestly don't know what I would do without my best friend!
She is just AMAZING!

# New year's resolution

*A post from 03.01.16*
*This was the first time I opened up to the world about my struggle.*

Here goes...
My New Year's resolution is to not be ashamed of who I am and to help others, so now is the time to share a little bit about the past year. For the past six months, I have been in hospital recovering from an eating disorder.

Throughout this time I have had so much support from friends and family and I couldn't be more grateful for that!! I am determined to beat this illness and I am not going to give in!! In 2 months time, I will finally be discharged from the unit and although I will not be fully recovered, I will be heading in the right direction.

For a long time, I have kept this a secret from a lot of people because I was ashamed of having an eating disorder, but now I want to use my experiences to help others and to show people that recovery is possible and there is life out there beyond and after an eating disorder!!

For those who are struggling, please don't give up!!
Granted it is hard and feels impossible at times, but trust me, it is so worth it!! Stay strong and keep going!!

# Squash

*A post from 30.01.16*
*This was the day I was allowed to start playing squash*
*again. It was such a huge achievement in my recovery.*

This morning, for the first time in 9 months, I was
allowed to go to squash training - and this time it was purely for fun
and not ED related!!
The past few months haven't been easy but this alone has made the
long journey to recovery worth it!! Every day brings a new challenge
but every day I am getting stronger and not allowing my eating
disorder to take over any more of my life.

# Remember how Anorexia makes you feel:

*A diary entry from 06.04.16*

*During a time when I was struggling, it helped me to write about all of the negative effects Anorexia had on me. This helped me to stay strong and fight my eating disorder.*

★ Going to bed each night, fearing that you won't wake up the next day.

★ Feeling upset when you see that your friends and family are upset.

★ Nothing you do is ever good enough for Anorexia, so it just makes you feel bad about yourself.

★ You felt even more different and isolated from people your age because you couldn't do the things they could.

★ Frustrated because you couldn't live a life you valued.

★ Out of control when you wanted to be in control.

★ Guilty (even if you follow Anorexia's rules).

★ Physically ill (cold, tired, hungry, lethargic, weak, numb).

# Rose Anne's Page of Positivity

*A diary entry from 14.08.16*
*I wrote this entry as an encouragement after struggling*
*during the weeks leading up to moving to university.*

★ You've met lots of nice people on your course and they are a great group to be with

★ You've worked so hard over the past year to reach your goal of going to uni, so don't let Anorexia ruin your progress with only 3 weeks to go!

★ Having a structured routine at uni will be very helpful for you and it will have a positive impact on your recovery. Remember how peaceful York makes you feel.

★ BELIEVE IN YOURSELF

★ The more you doubt yourself, the stronger Anorexia will become.

★ Remember everything you can do and achieve if you live a life YOU want to rather than following the rules of the eating disorder:

- Join sports clubs at uni
- Better concentration
- Join in with meals out/takeaways with friends at uni
- Be a positive influence to others
- Continue being a Time To Change Young Champion
- Pursue your ambition of becoming a psychologist

# I want to be 'normal'

*A diary entry from 19.08.16*
*At the time of writing this, I was beginning to pick myself*
*up after having a blip. It was a difficult time, as I felt*
*overwhelmed by the voice of Anorexia.*

So this week has gone well recovery wise, but I'm scared.
I'm putting on a brave face, eating my meals and snacks and
avoiding the scales.

But I have no idea how long I can keep this up!

I just keep trying to tell myself that I need to restore my weight so
that I can stay at uni. However, every single time, Anorexia fights
back and tells me not to gain weight because if I do, people at uni
won't like me. The more I eat, the worse I feel and the harder it
becomes. I just feel like everything I eat is building up inside and it's
all going to stay there and make me gain weight.

Why is this so difficult?? I just want to be 'normal' and free.
I'm finally starting to do things that people my age are doing, such
as moving out and going to university.

But anorexia tries to stop me from doing these things. The only way
I can continue to do what my peers do is to not listen to Anorexia.
That's going to be really difficult and exhausting, but it'll be worth it
in the end.

# Holiday of a lifetime

*A post from 23.08.16*
*This is the wonderful*
*moment when I*
*realised it is worth*
*fighting for recovery if*
*it means you can have*
*times like this.*

Wow!!
So after FOUR YEARS of
planning on going to
France together, we have
finally done it!!
Relaxing in the sun with
my best friend seems like a
world away from this time
last year in the unit, unable to even go outside, never mind to another
country!

I say 'we' have done it, because I know that I wouldn't be in this
position without Alice by my side as well as the endless support of
family and friends. This is by no means the end of my road to
recovery, but it is another step in the right direction and a milestone I
never imagined I would reach so quickly!

Sometimes you just have to hold on to the hope that things can get
better and you'll be able to live your life without being controlled by
your illness!

## 33

# Keep Fighting

*This entry was about encouraging myself to not give in to my eating disorder.*

The way I'm feeling is so hard to explain. Anorexia is very loud because I'm fighting back. But somehow, I still seem to be stronger than Anorexia , because it is not having an impact on my intake. I'm trying so hard to fight and it's making me really tired, but it's definitely worth it!
There's one thing I'm certain of:
I HAVE TO KEEP FIGHTING!
I HAVE TO KEEP FIGHTING!
I HAVE TO KEEP FIGHTING!

# I am beginning to feel 'normal' again

*A diary entry from 06.11.16*
*How being at university has really helped me to fight for a life without Anorexia.*

What I'm about to write about occurred to me at 1am this morning and I feel it's a really important point to get across.

All of my life, I have felt somewhat different from other people. Not completely, but in a more subtle sense. I have longed to fully fit in somewhere, whether at school or outside of education. In a way, maybe Anorexia was a means of coping with these feelings of not being like other people. But my point here is, it is not 'normal' to isolate yourself from the world, nor is it 'normal' to turn down meals with your friends because you're scared of the food and scared of being judged. It seems like what was meant to be a way of coping actually led me to feel even more different to my peers.

But today, I offered to bring the post-game cakes for our squash match at uni. Making them was actually quite therapeutic and then that evening, I suddenly realised how 'normal' I felt. We each played our opponent and then after a hard game of squash, we all sat down and had a slice of cake. Whereas before, I would have done everything to avoid that situation, I challenged my eating disorder and subsequently felt good for having joined in. And all of this was possible because I didn't let anorexia get the better of me.

# Moving away from my meal plan

*A diary entry from 21.11.16*
*There came a point in my recovery where I felt able to veer away from my meal plan and this is how it felt.*

I've recently decided to take the big step of not strictly following a meal plan any more. My mind set has vastly improved, to the point where I'm in a much better place mentally, which is great!

To start with, I found the change quite difficult to deal with, because Anorexia felt out of control. Nothing was certain anymore and so my ED tried to keep a mental note of exactly what I had eaten in the day. But the more I listened to my body instead, Anorexia began to quieten. I do sometimes find myself adding up calories in my head, but the meaning of them has changed.

Food and calories are no longer my arch enemy, but my friend and necessity. Whereas before, the meaning of calories, fats, sugars etc provoked fear and anxiety in me, they now denote fuel, life and freedom. Anorexia is now the enemy, not the friend.

# Realisation about hunger

*A diary entry from 15.12.16*
*This was a very recent discovery, but one which has been crucial in my Recovery. This is one of the things that has helped me to stay well.*

I've been feeling really hungry recently and it made me realise something ...

Before now, I would feel hungry and get scared that I would eat non stop and therefore gain lots of weight. I Ignored the hunger, which eventually led me to restrict and then relapse. And every time, the same thing would happen. This extreme hunger would return once I was near to reaching my target weight.

So now it's time for a new approach. I will listen to my body and give it what it wants and needs. If I'm hungry, I will eat and soon my weight will even out and my body will find a weight that suits it. There's no point going round in circles any more because that won't get me anywhere.

Anorexia will still try to make me react to feelings of guilt, but I'm not going to give in. I am not going to forfeit my recovery and therefore my life just for a slightly slimmer-looking body. It's not worth it and I am so much more than my appearance. I am happy with who I am and the person I have become so I won't allow Anorexia to take that from me. Instead I will feel the fear and do it anyway!!

# Christmas Day

*A diary entry from 25.12.16*
*I wrote this entry after having a very encouraging and enjoyable Christmas day with my family. It really helped me to see how far I have come in such a short space of time.*

Today is the day that we celebrate the birth of Jesus. It is a time to love, a time of joy and a time of hope.

Last Christmas I was still in hospital, but I was allowed overnight leave so I could spend Christmas Day with my family.
At the time, things seemed to go really well, which they did in such circumstances. But a year on, I can see how far I have come in my recovery.

I remember still being very much controlled by Anorexia, especially on Christmas Day.

It got the better of me when dishing out our own food, as my portion sizes were a bit on the small side and the thought of not having a meal plan was completely incomprehensible at the time.

However, I now feel much more in control and I'm able to eat what I want when I want without having to follow a strict meal plan. This year, I probably ate slightly more than I would on a typical day, but that's ok! After all, Christmas is a time to love (which includes loving yourself) and my body deserves to feel full and nourished. For the first time in quite a while, it actually felt as if I didn't have an eating disorder and instead, the niggling thoughts were just similar to the ones that other people might also encounter. Instead of my main focus being on food like it was last year, I began to look from a different perspective and realised that the most important thing on Christmas Day is to give thanks to God for the birth of his son, rather than focussing solely on food.

# Boxing Day

*A diary entry from 26.12.16*
*This was written after having a good few weeks in terms of recovery. It helps me to stay focused and realise that squash is a massive motivator to get better.*

It's Boxing Day today and this morning, Dad asked if I wanted to play squash. I hadn't played for a couple of weeks, so of course I said I'd love to! Whereas before I would have avoided eating, I made sure I had a substantial breakfast so I had enough energy on court. When anorexia was in control, exercise (even squash) was a punishment, a way of burning calories and a means to lose weight. It was no longer fun or enjoyable, it was just a pure obsession.

However, my decision to play squash today was not because of some voice in my head telling me I need to exercise to lose weight, but because I wanted to reward myself for all of my hard work. I had given my body the energy it needed, not only on Christmas Day, but in the weeks leading up to it, and so my body gave me recognition of that by giving me the energy to run around the court. Nowadays, squash is a fun, rewarding and stress-relieving activity which I play because I WANT to and not because I HAVE to.

# Feeling Trapped

*This drawing shows many of the different thoughts that Anorexia made me feel.*

Starting from the middle, I wrote 'HELP", because I felt trapped and unable to escape these anorexic thoughts. The crossed out words are ones which anorexia promised I would be, but in fact, I didn't feel strong, proud or happy at all!

Then comes the words which are actually how anorexia made me feel. Note that these are all negative feelings. On the outside are reasons anorexia gave me not to recover and therefore some of the things that sometimes stopped me from choosing recovery.

# Fight for your life

*This picture shows how loud Anorexia can be compared to 'Rose Anne'.*

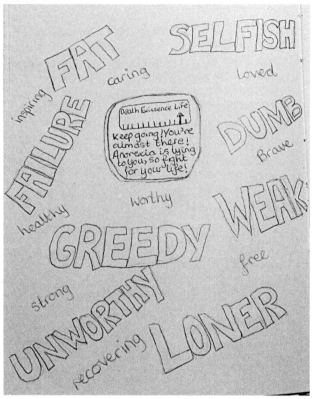

When I was nearly at my target weight, I found that my anorexic thoughts were often very strong. This drawing helped me to explain that, although I was nearly weight restored, Anorexia's voice was still much louder than my own.

But I still knew deep down that anorexia was lying to me, so restoring my weight would actually help to quieten the intrusive thoughts and allow me to live a life that I value.

The more I paid attention to the lower-case words, the bigger they would become and the smaller the upper-case ones would get.

# Measuring my achievements

*At times when I have urges to weigh myself, I look back to this drawing in my diary and it helps me to alter my focus.*

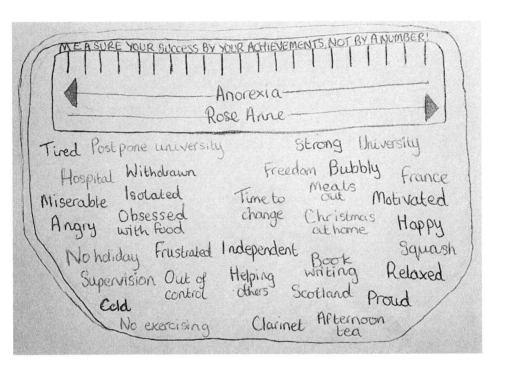

Many people say that our weight is irrelevant when measuring your success. But I like to go a step further and say that actually, when my BMI is higher, I seem to get more fulfilment from life. I am much more able to do things I enjoy, such as travelling and studying at university. In short, for every bit of weight I restore, I also seem to gain back a part of my personality or my life.

# Distorted image

*I did this drawing to try to explain what Anorexia says I look like compared to other people.*

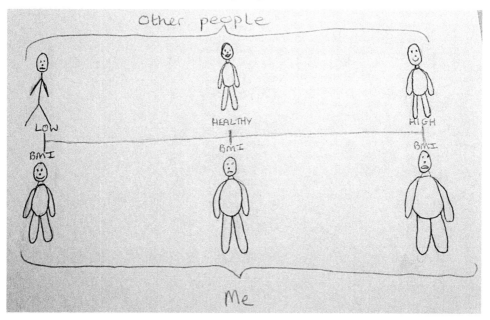

Anorexia's perception of how I look is that statistically, I would have to be at a significantly lower weight to appear a similar size to someone else of normal weight.

Also notice the facial expressions of each person - the ones which represent me gradually get happier as the weight goes down, whereas the other people are happiest at a healthy weight. My eating disorder tells me that I will be happier if I lose weight but deep down, I know this is not the case.

These days, I take a different approach to how I view my body. Instead of allowing emotions to become involved, I try to just think about the facts, which are usually very positive.

**44**

For example, whereas before, I may not have liked the way my legs looked and therefore focused on the negative things about them, I can look at them now and see that they are actually a fascinating feature of my body. I write down a list of these things, so I can look back and reflect. Here is the list about my legs.

The facts about your legs:

- ★ They enable you to walk
- ★ You have knees so you can bend down
- ★ Your feet allow you to control the pedals in the car
- ★ You can tap your feet to enjoyable music
- ★ Having toes means you can decorate your toenails in all sorts of different colours and patterns.

Notice that these are all positive things and the list includes activities which I enjoy doing. It brings me to the realisation that if my legs weren't there, I wouldn't be able to do many of the things I enjoy doing. Because of this, I always come to the conclusion that I would prefer for me to sometimes have body image issues surrounding my legs than to not have them at all.

# Wisdom for warriors

This section is aimed at people who are struggling with an eating disorder. However, many of the techniques mentioned are also useful for a good mental wellbeing.

# Therapy

*New to therapy? Here's a bit about what to expect, as well as how therapy has helped me during my recovery.*

I'll never forget a conversation I had with one of the hospital staff, during which I was explaining that I didn't feel I was ill enough and felt guilty for taking up a bed. But he reminded me of the fact a team of specialists agreed that I needed to be admitted and that meant I was 'ill enough' and did need help. So many people have similar feelings about them not being 'ill enough' or not having an eating disorder, but that doesn't mean that these feelings are true. Something I learnt from therapy is that feelings are not facts. This doesn't mean that your feelings are not important or valid, it just means that, although you may feel a certain way, the facts may say otherwise. (Like if a person feels fat but statistically, they are a healthy weight.)

One thing I would also like to say is that if you are experiencing symptoms of an eating disorder, don't be afraid to ask for help. Getting support as soon as possible will give you the best chance of a full recovery (although that's certainly not to say that those who have been battling an eating disorder for a long time cannot recover!!) Being over a certain weight or BMI does not make your difficulty any less significant or less important!! At the end of the day, eating disorders are mental illnesses and are not solely defined by what you weigh. There is no such thing as 'not ill enough' and you ALL deserve help and freedom from your eating disorder!!

<u>Outpatients</u>

Receiving help for the first time can be daunting for a number of reasons. Maybe you're worried you might not get on with your therapist, you're conscious of what other people might think, or maybe you don't feel you deserve or need help.

Whatever the reasons, it is very common and in fact normal to be having these thoughts. I think the fact that this was an entirely new and unfamiliar experience to me is the reason I was apprehensive. But despite these anxieties, I knew that therapy was going to be important if I wanted to get my life back. At first, I did find it difficult to open up, because I'd never properly talked to anyone about my feelings before. But in time, I started to trust my therapist and became more open and honest with her.

I think the difficulty with eating disorders is that, not only is there the psychological issue, but there is also sometimes a risk with a person's physical well being. I've come to realise that at times when my physical health was deteriorating, my therapy sessions concentrated more on food, weight and what I could do to get back on track.

However, when I am on top of my eating disorder and am physically healthier, we're able to tackle the underlying issues, which in turn helps to lessen the need for me to use Anorexia as a coping mechanism.

During your first session, it is likely that your therapist will want to get to know you a bit and find out about your background and current difficulties. You might also discuss what you would like to get out of therapy and decide on any goals you want to set. And remember, YOU are the one in the driving seat, so, although your therapist might have some suggestions, you are the one who ultimately decides what you cover in each session.

Here are a few tips on how to make the most of therapy:

★ Try to think about what you might like to talk about/go through in each session.

★ Everything you say is valid - nothing will sound silly or stupid to your therapist.

★ For the best outcome, it is  important to practice the things you learn in therapy in your everyday life. The more you practice, the more natural it will become.

★ Even if your first session didn't go as well as you hoped, try a few more sessions first. If it still doesn't seem helpful, try to determine why. It may be that you might gel better with a different therapist, or a different therapeutic approach.

Daycare

To ease the transition between inpatient and outpatient treatment, I attended daycare for around 2 months. It is open from Monday to Friday, although the number of days each patient attends varies.

Because the hospital was quite far away from my house, I attended twice a week. It would open at 8am and we would generally all have breakfast and lunch together.

The difference with daycare was that, although supported, there was much more freedom and in some respects, each patient held more responsibility over managing their own meal plan.

I still received weekly therapy and was also assigned a support worker who I could talk to whenever I needed to. I tried to use the two days at daycare to challenge my eating disorder, as the staff were there to support us and to discuss how we felt the challenge had gone.

Because there were the same three members of staff at daycare, I was able to build a closer relationship with them and it therefore became a lot easier for me to talk about how I was feeling.

As I have mentioned before, everyone is different, however daycare has been extremely useful for me and I would definitely recommend it if you are given the opportunity to attend day patient treatment.

Inpatients

Being admitted to hospital can be extremely scary and anxiety-provoking, because you know you'll inevitably be facing your fear and going head-to-head with your eating disorder. Every unit is different, so it's difficult to say exactly what it will be like, but here is my experience of being in hospital:

When I first arrived, the staff took me to my room and checked my belongings to make sure I didn't have any banned items. Once I had unpacked my things, the RMN (Registered Mental Health Nurse) took my physical observations (blood pressure, temperature etc.) and then I was taken to the lounge and introduced to the other 9 patients. As I was 18, I was on an adult ward, so there was a fairly big age range. This is what a general day on the unit would look like:

8am - 8.30am: medication and physical observations
8.30am - 9am: breakfast
9am - 10am: rest period
10am - 10:30am: group/free time
10:30am - 10:45am: morning snack
10:45am - 11:15am: rest period
11:15am - 12:00pm: group/15 min grounds walk/free time
12:00pm - 12:30pm: lunch
12:30pm - 1:30pm: rest period
1:30pm - 2:30pm: group/free time
2:30pm - 2:45pm: afternoon snack
2:45pm - 3:15pm: rest period
3:15pm - 5:00pm: group/access/free time
5:00pm - 5:45pm: evening meal
5:45pm - 6:45pm: rest period
6:45pm - 8:00pm: free time
8:00pm - 8:30pm: evening snack
8:30pm - 9pm: rest period

**51**

We had both individual and group therapy throughout the week and there were also certain creative groups, such as card making or painting, which helped to keep us occupied during the day.

As patients progressed, they were gradually allowed time away from the unit. To start with, this access was supervised, but eventually we were allowed unsupervised access (for me, this was generally one hour twice a week).

When I got closer to my discharge date, I was allowed overnight leave. I remember my very first night at home. I didn't have much time, but the little time I had meant the world to me, especially since it was the day of the yearly 'rushbearing' event at my church. I have to admit, I faced many challenges whilst on home leave, mainly because whilst in hospital, all of the control over and responsibility for my meals was with the chef, whereas when I went home, much of it was given back to me.

Despite the difficulties of being at home, every little step towards recovery is what ultimately led me to being well enough to be discharged from hospital. Even just taking a bit less time eating a meal or trying something that I had not allowed myself to eat for a while were things which were all a step in the right direction.

As I had been away from home for a few months, my family saw a huge difference even on my first home leave. They said I appeared a lot calmer and less anxious around mealtimes, although they could also tell that it was still very difficult for me. Seeing my family happy and proud made me feel good about myself too and maybe even a little proud.

**52**

# Letter of encouragement during difficult times

*I wrote this letter to help me to look back and reflect on how much my life has changed for the better since I started my journey to recovery. It is aimed at my younger self as an encouragement to keep going when I was really struggling to fight against my eating disorder.*
*I hope this can also help you to see that there is hope and you can overcome this. So this letter is also for you:*

Dear friend,
Firstly, I want you to know that you will get the help you need and things will get better!! Please don't give up, because this illness isn't going to take over your whole life. It's also important that you know this isn't your fault and you do deserve to be free!!

I know you're struggling at the moment, even though you won't personally admit it, but just remember that so many people out there care about you and the only person you're being dishonest with is yourself.

Don't allow the illness to torture you and then pretend everything is fine, because deep down you know that it isn't.
This is going to be a tough journey, but you are strong enough to battle through it!! You'll learn to allow yourself to feel the anxiety and to not avoid the situations which trigger such anxiety.

I know at this moment in time, you see no way out and it seems like your eating disorder is your only hope, but please realise that it is

**53**

lying to you!! It will not make you happier, you won't be satisfied with your next 'target weight' and it certainly won't resolve your problems. You will also no longer have any control, because your eating disorder will have taken that from you as well.

So all I am going to say is that your sheer determination is what will help you in your recovery. It will take a long time to fully recover and you will have blips along the way, but one bad day does not mean that you are relapsing; it just means you're living a normal life and although today isn't great, tomorrow can be better.

Recovery is what you make it to be!! Although it would be great to have no intrusive thoughts (especially around body image and food), that may not necessarily be the case. However, learning to manage these thoughts is the key to living a happy and healthy life and living a life that you value.
So please don't give up! You're allowed to be kind to yourself and realise that once you're on the road to recovery, you can do so much more!

Everything just seems more fun and enjoyable and trust me, it's worth all of the anxiety you have to endure in order to get your life back!
At times when you're finding things difficult, please read this letter to assure you that you can and will get through this difficult time.

Onwards and upwards,

R.A.E xx

# Distress Tolerance

*We can use distress tolerance at times when we are unable to solve the problem and/or we are not currently in a flexible mind-set. There are 4 different aspects to distress tolerance.*
*These are: Distraction, Self-Soothing, Improving the Moment and Pros & Cons.*

Wise mind ACCEPTS

The first part of distress tolerance is to use the ACCEPTS acronym to help to distract you from these distressing thoughts until you are able to rationally deal with them.

The acronym helps to show different things to help to distract you. These are:

★ Activities:
  - Participate in hobbies which you enjoy doing such as painting or playing video games.

★ Contributing:
  - Do something for others such as volunteering.

★ Comparisons:
  - If you are coping better with a certain situation now, make the comparison. (Please note – comparison doesn't suit everyone, so if it doesn't help, skip this one out).

★ Emotions:
-    Distract yourself with something that will give you the opposite emotion to how you're feeling. E.g. if you're feeling sad, watch something that will make you laugh.

★ Thoughts:
-    Temporarily distract yourself by pushing away the distressing thoughts.
-    Maybe try to imagine putting these thoughts into a box and locking the padlock. You can bring your attention to them at a later time.

★ Sensations:
-    Distract yourself with other sensations such as listening to loud music.

**56**

Self soothing

Using self soothing techniques allows us to feel calmer, comforted and just generally more relaxed. It is important to use these techniques at times when you are not distressed and when you are feeling more positive, so that when you do NEED to use distress tolerance, it just comes to you naturally. This does take time, but the more you practice, the easier it becomes.

Self soothing includes all five of the senses:

★ Vision:
   -   Look at something which makes you feel relaxed. It may be somewhere outside around nature, or even a picture which brings back positive memories.

★ Sound:
   -   Listen to some relaxing music or sounds which you find comforting. Try to be mindful when listening to the music. Allow the sounds to come and go and if the music has lyrics, focus on them.

★ Smell:
   -   Try to notice the smells around you. Maybe go outside and smell all of the different flowers around. Or light a candle and analyse the smell.

★ Taste:
   -   Herbal tea can be great for self soothing.

★ Touch:
   -   Find an object with an interesting texture.

## Self-soothe box

A self soothe box is a really useful and positive coping mechanism when you are struggling to think rationally and you're finding things difficult. It also acts as an alternative to the more harmful and negative ways of coping that we may have developed.

One thing I found really helpful was to make a self soothe box, so at times of distress and anxiety, I am able to use the items in the box to calm me down and help me to relax. Here is what my self-soothe box looks like:

IMPROVE the moment

This technique helps us to get through a particularly difficult moment. We use the acronym IMPROVE to remember the different stages of this activity. These are:

★ Imagery:
- What imagery do you find the most useful?

★ Meaning:
- What phrase could you use to remind you to look for meaning in difficult situations?

★ Prayer:
- What prayer, poem or quote might help you to accept a difficult situation?
(This doesn't have to be a religious thing, it's just something that speaks to you)

★ Relaxation:
- What type of relaxation do you find the most effective?

★ One thing at a time:
- What exercise or activity will help you to stay in the here and now?

★ Vacation:
- What activity or person helps you to have time out when you need it?

★ Encouragement:
- What phrase could you use to give yourself encouragement?

**59**

This is the IMPROVE design I made to help me get through difficult moments.

**Imagery**

My 'safe place' is on the top of a hill in the countryside. Imagining myself here instantly makes me feel calm.

**Relaxation**

Prayer (and mindfulness) are two things that help to relax me and clear my mind.

**Vacation**

Going walking or cycling helps to free my mind. This in itself is a motivation for me, as I can only do these 2 activities when I am well.

**Meaning**

A quote from Winnie the Pooh which helps me to get through times of anxiety and stress.

**Prayer**

Lyrics from an inspirational song written by a well known Christian musician.

**One Thing At A Time**

When playing or listening to music, I get a sense of freedom and I am able to concentrate solely on the music and/or lyrics of the song.

**Encouragement**

Since I love nature and the countryside, this quote really inspires me to keep moving forward.

## Using pros and cons

Using pros and cons is a great way to help us to make a decision, especially when we are not necessarily in flexible mind to start with, as it allows time for our emotions to settle down and allows us to think more rationally and sensibly. Here, we asses a situation but find  the pros and cons of tolerating the distress with not tolerating it. We might use an example of deciding whether or not to carry out an old but more negative coping strategy versus using a new coping strategy.

Here's how to structure the pros and cons:

My basic choices are ..............................
versus...................................

| Short-term pros of ...................... | Short-term cons of ...................... |
|---|---|
|  |  |
| Long-term pros of ...................... | Long term cons of ...................... |
|  |  |
| Versus | |

| Short-term pros of .................... | Short-term cons of .................... |
|---|---|
| | |
| Long-term pros of .................... | Long term cons of .................... |
| | |

**63**

## Radical Acceptance

Radical acceptance is a skill which allows us to cope with painful situations which are difficult to accept.

- ★ Notice the sensations in your body

- ★ Freedom from suffering requires acceptance from deep within of what is.

- ★ Pain creates suffering only when you refuse to ACCEPT the pain.

- ★ Deciding to tolerate the moment is ACCEPTANCE.

- ★ Accepting something doesn't mean you agree with it or approve of it, it is just acknowledging the situation.

- ★ You will have to commit to acceptance over and over again, but the more you do it, the easier it becomes.

I found radical acceptance extremely difficult to start with, because accepting pain is hard for anybody to do. But this is a skill which is worth developing, as I have found that acceptance is the key to reducing your suffering.

Once I accepted that I felt a certain way in certain situations (i.e. anxious around food), I was able to find a way to help me when I was faced with those situations. I used skills such as mindfulness and distress tolerance (in particular distraction techniques) to make it easier to battle through these feelings. The more I was able to do this, the easier and less anxiety-provoking these situations became.

## Willingness

Willingness is about doing just what is needed in a situation. It includes:

★ Focusing on effectiveness.

★ Listening very carefully to your wise mind.

★ Acting from your inner self (doing what YOU want to do/know is the 'right' thing)

## Wilfulness

Wilfulness should be replaced with willingness, as wilfulness is not effective and won't get you to where you want to be. It means:

★ Not doing anything when action is needed.

★ Giving up.

★ Trying to FIX every situation.

★ Refusing to TOLERATE the moment.

# Mindfulness

There are so many misconceptions as to what mindfulness actually is. Although meditation can be a part of mindfulness, it is not the only component.

So what is mindfulness?

★ Living in the present moment.

★ Taking the present moment as it is and not judging it.

# How to be mindful

Observe the situation:

- ★ Notice the sensations in your body.

- ★ Purposefully pay attention to the present moment.

- ★ Accept the emotion. Don't push anything away and don't cling to anything.

- ★ Allow thoughts to come into your mind and then slowly fade away.

Describe:

- ★ Put words on the experience.

- ★ Label what you observe.

- ★ Distinguish between thought and fact.

- ★ Take away your own opinions and work only with the facts.

Participate:

- ★ Throw yourself completely into the activities of the current moment.

- ★ Use wise mind when completing tasks.

- ★ Go with the flow.

**67**

Don't make judgements:

- ★ Don't evaluate the situation as good or bad.

- ★ Accept each moment.

- ★ Acknowledge your values and your reactions to the situation, but don't judge them.

Don't multitask:

- ★ Direct your full attention to the present moment.

- ★ Do one thing at a time.

- ★ Ignore distractions.

- ★ Concentrate your mind.

Be effective:

- ★ BELIEVE IN YOURSELF

- ★ Participate fully.

- ★ Be open minded.

- ★ Stay away from judging things as 'right' or 'wrong'.

## States of mind

There are three different states of mind (mind-sets) which all serve a different purpose, however being in a certain mind-set in a certain situation might be a hindrance to you.

The three different states of mind are:

- ★ Fixed mind – Where a person is not willing to adapt to change and is set with what they think is 'right'.

- ★ Fatalistic mind – Where a person tends to catastrophize and they believe that there is no way out and no hope.

- ★ Flexible mind – Where a person is more easily adaptable to change and they are open to new experiences. They don't allow past experiences or future worries to influence them and they concentrate on the present moment.

After learning about the different mind-sets, I found it useful to simply recognise what mind-set I was in in certain situations. Even if I couldn't change my mind-set at the time, just being able to know which state of mind I was in allowed me to reflect on the situation later on (when I was in flexible mind-set and my actions weren't driven by anxiety).

This then means I can try to problem solve and work out a way to improve the situation next time by putting certain plans or procedures in place (e.g. doing a list of the pros and cons of acting on the thought).

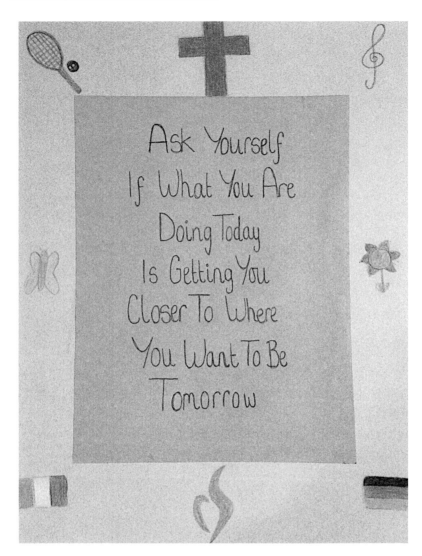

Ask Yourself
If What You Are
Doing Today
Is Getting You
Closer To Where
You Want To Be
Tomorrow

70

Acceptance and commitment therapy looks at your values and what kind of person you want to be.

When your eating disorder thoughts are strong, it helps you to concentrate on the things you value the most and the person you want to be.

To start with, think about the things you value the most. For example, my main values are to be loving and caring to everyone I meet, to be a follower of Jesus and to help others who are suffering from Anorexia Nervosa.

If Anorexia is shouting at me to not eat a certain food or to restrict in any way, I will think back to the underlying question of 'will this action bring you closer or further away from living a life according to your values?

Generally, the outcome is that I have to look after myself in order to care for others and I am also only able to help other sufferers if I am in a good position both mentally and physically. Seeing as my studies are important to me, I tell myself that my ability to concentrate and to learn will be much better if I let go of my eating disorder.

So try to think about the things you value the most, so that next time anorexia is trying to trick you into following its rules, you are more equipped to fight back and win the battle.

# Taking the Leap

*This picture is a metaphor for facing your fear in order to move closer to where you truly want to be.*

In recovery from Anorexia, there are lots of times when you may be afraid to take a step towards recovery and this might just help to explain:

The tent on the right indicates the fact that you can just about survive at this side of the moat and it's where you feel comfortable, but all of your dreams are actually across the water, in the castle.

The only way you can get there is by going across the rickety bridge and risk falling into the water. But you want so desperately to have the freedom that the castle gives you and so you eventually decide to 'take the leap'.

It may be that you stumble whilst on the bridge however, you are able to pick yourself up and get closer to the castle.

This is what recovery feels like. It's about trying, stumbling, getting back on your feet, not giving up and most importantly, believing in yourself.

No matter how old you are or how long you've been fighting, you can recover and you deserve to live a life free from your eating disorder.

So don't wait until tomorrow. The longer you wait, the harder it is to make that first step. Start today and keep on going until you reach your own personal castle.

# Dear Body of mine

*During one of my group therapy sessions, we were encouraged to write a letter to our bodies as if we were apologising to a friend. Here is the letter I wrote.*

Dear body of mine,

It is so difficult to sum up our relationship. As a young child, I was very accepting of you and, to be honest, we were on quite good terms! I didn't care about your weight, nor did I feel negative about certain parts of you. I wore what I wanted and didn't mind that other people thought my sense of style was odd. But why did that all change?

The truth is, you were always the one who was there for me – you literally are the thing that keeps me alive and you've helped me to achieve so much. You are the reason I managed to complete my Duke of Edinburgh Award, you enabled me to play the clarinet and to be honest, you're the reason I can live the life I want to.

But I shoved all of that back in your face and paid too much attention to other people's negative comments. I listened to them instead of sticking up for you. I changed the clothes you found extremely comfortable, because others didn't like them and then, when I still felt different, I began to abuse you even more. I deprived you of the most important thing that you need in order to function and I thought that was acceptable!! I tortured you, made you exercise when you had no fuel, all of the hurt the bullies caused me was pushed on to you and, in effect, I became a bully to you. And all of this happened just because I wanted to be liked and accepted by others. But thankfully, you were strong and kept on going regardless!!

For a long time, our relationship has been one-sided: you gave everything and I gave nothing back. That is something we have in common. But the difference was, you couldn't break free from our relationship. You were trapped and the only way you could have escaped would have been to give up. And I'd now like to thank you for keeping going!

I have taken the decision to make our relationship more even. I want to be your friend and I now accept both you and myself for what we truly are. I accept that we're not going to be the thinnest or the prettiest and that sometimes people might talk about you or your clothes in a negative way. But now I know there is no such thing as perfect. One person's perfect is not the same as someone else's. And surely it is better for people to get to know the real me, rather than trying to pretend to be someone or something that I'm not.

I don't seem to have the same perception of you as other people, but now I accept that all those people who say you look great now you're weight restored can't have all been lying and maybe it is MY view that is distorted.

I may never see your true beauty, but I accept you and now I see you as more than just a weight or a size, but instead I see strength, endurance and courage. So thank you for putting up with all of the pain and suffering I forced upon you. From now on, I promise I will look after you, be kind to you and treat you with love and respect.

Lots of love and thank you, Rose Anne.

# Your body is your friend

*A visual aid which helps me to think of myself as a friend to my body.*

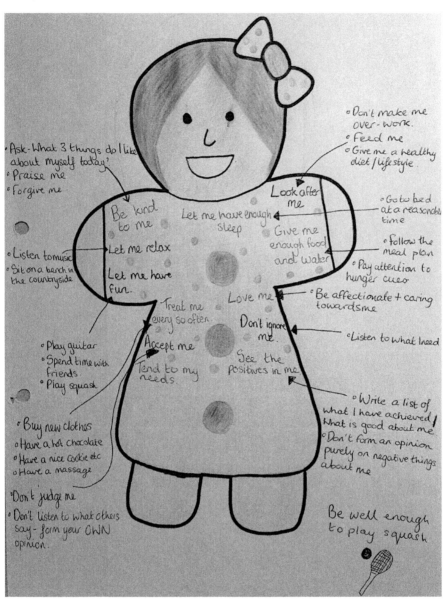

When doing this drawing, I firstly thought about how I treat my friends, or what I would advise my friends to do to look after themselves. In a way, it's my guide on how to be kind to myself and look after my body. Having this separate image allows me to take a step back and reflect on whether or not I am being a good friend to my body.

It struck me that this is how I would like other people to treat me (accept me for who I am and seeing the positives in me). But it occurred to me that I couldn't expect other people to do this if I wasn't being kind to myself. I decided that this had to change because, although I was looking after others, I wasn't taking care of myself. I realised that if I did the latter, then I would also be more able to help my friends and family.

# Helping your loved one

When someone is suffering with an eating disorder, their condition can also have a huge impact on their loved ones. This section is designed for people who know someone who has an eating disorder and aims to give an insight into how the person may be feeling and to provide tips on how to help.

# Supporting a friend

If you suspect your friend may have an eating disorder, talking to them about it for the first time can be very daunting. But please don't be afraid to start a conversation with them, because just knowing someone cares could mean the world to a person who is silently battling an eating disorder.

Here are a few tips that may help you, but please bear in mind that everyone is different and what works for some people won't necessarily work for all.

★ Choose a suitable place and time to speak to your friend - it would be better to be somewhere where you're not likely to be disturbed and have plenty of time to talk.

★ To begin with, your friend may be reluctant to talk. It is ok if you have some silences during your conversation.

★ Give the person time to open up - don't force them into saying anything they don't feel comfortable talking about.

★ Your friend might experience a number of different feelings and emotions when you talk to them about your concerns. This may be displayed through anger or denial, but please realise that this is not aimed directly at you.

★ Let them know that they are able to trust you and you'll be there to for them along the way.

**79**

# The importance of friendship

Eating disorders can make a person feel very isolated and lonely, even if people around them are very supportive. It may take time for that person to see beyond their eating disorder and to see that they do have people around them who care.

## My Best friend Alice

I cannot begin to explain how much my best friend Alice has helped me throughout my recovery. During my time in hospital, she kept in regular contact with me and sent letters and drawings of what we were going to do together when I was discharged from hospital. These gave me hope and made me realise that there was light at the end of the tunnel. To Alice, these were just little things but to me, they were the highlight of my day and were often the reason I would give myself to keep fighting.

I know when I first told Alice that I had Anorexia, she felt guilty about not knowing or realising that something was wrong. But if this is something you are struggling with, I can assure you that you are not to blame! Anorexia is such a secretive and deceiving illness and it changes the person's personality and rids them of their values. Just because they have kept quiet, it doesn't mean they don't trust your, nor does it mean they don't want to tell you. Anorexia also distorts a person's view, so they may not think they have an issue to begin with.

Alice drew this for me during my admission. It was a very lovely and personal gift to receive and it helped me to see how many positive things I could do if I carried on recovering.

## Writing letters

Once I started to receive therapy, I realised that it was easier for me to write down how I was feeling as opposed to talking to someone face to face. So, I decided to write a letter to my best friend Alice to explain how I felt and to thank her for being there for me. Within a couple of days, Alice had replied and it turns out that writing was a lot easier than talking for her too. From then on, we have written numerous letters to each other and I feel this has brought us even closer together.

## Hope for the future

Once I started to get home leave from hospital, I sometimes visited Alice at university. It was her first year at the time and it really helped me to see how amazing university life was and gave me something to aim for.

I already had my place secured at The University of York for the following year, so I knew that if I continued to get better, I would also be able to go to university and Alice would then be able to visit me too!

And, just like I did for her, she came and helped me to move in to my new accommodation. She helped me put up my fairy lights and all of my encouragement posters that I had made in hospital and, before I knew it, my room felt like home.

## University

Starting university is daunting for everybody, but it can be particularly challenging for those suffering from an eating disorder. No matter how long a person has been in recovery, a big change, such as moving to university, can often lead them to fall back on unhelpful behaviours, such as restriction. University can also be a place where a person might develop an eating disorder, so being aware of this may help them to get help more quickly.

Since coming to uni, my flatmates have been so supportive. I told them about my eating disorder quite early on and if ever I am struggling, they'll give me a helping hand. For example, I sometimes struggle when there are people in the kitchen who I don't know. If this is the case, I often get flustered and can't think rationally.

On various occasions, I have asked my flatmates for some advice since they're able to think clearly and they suggested cooking something that I could leave in the oven and then when it's ready, I could eat in my room. Just little things like this can make a huge difference and proves that someone cares.

**83**

Only a few months ago, going to a cafe for tea and cake would have be extremely anxiety-provoking for me, because I found the atmosphere challenging, as well as the food being towards the 'scarier' end of my list of 'fear foods'.

However, this is now something I enjoy doing once a week with my flatmate Becky. I know that our cafe visits have helped me to not only become more decisive, but to also feel more relaxed in these kind of environments.

If you have a friend who is ready to take this step, my best advice would be to try to be as patient as possible with them. To start with, it took me a long time to calm myself down once I became anxious and that meant that I had difficulty choosing what to get. But because Becky was so patient with me, I gradually became a lot more decisive and started to feel so much more relaxed.

# Friend Q & A

Q: My friend is in an inpatient unit. Should I visit them?

A: There is no straight forward answer to this question. It's really a decision that both you and your friend have to make together. If you are able to visit and feel comfortable doing so, ask them if they would like you to go to see them. It may be that they say no to begin with, and this can be for many reasons. However, try not to take it personally because it might be that they just need a little time to adjust.

Q: What is the best way to help my friend?

A: Again, this varies from person to person. But the easiest way to find out is by asking. Ask them if there's anything you can do (or stop doing) in order to support them.

Q: Should I confront my friend if I see them carrying out ED behaviours?

A: My advice here would be that it is important that your friend knows that you want to help them to recover. Try not to overwhelm them with questions, but calmly ask them if their eating disorder is making the decision or if they are.
However you may not feel comfortable bringing up topics like this. If that is the case, that is perfectly fine and the best thing to do would be to talk to someone you trust about it. This may be a teacher or a parent, but it will allow you to share your concerns so you are not trying to take on too much at once.

Q: Can't my friend just eat?

A: To be honest, even I didn't understand why I couldn't 'just eat'. But thinking about it, it felt as if I was a puppet and Anorexia was controlling my strings. Asking me to 'just eat' was the same as asking me to face my biggest fear, which is why this statement made me really frustrated, mainly with myself. For me, Anorexia was a way of gaining control and therefore me giving in to hunger meant that I was losing that control.

# My Advice for friends

★ It is great that you want to be there for your friend, but above all, make sure to take care of yourself.

★ Try to avoid talking about dieting or weight around your friend, as this can be triggering for someone with an eating disorder.

★ If your friend has an eating disorder, doing a little bit of research about their condition will help you to gain a better understanding of how they are currently feeling.

★ Keep being yourself! Although there is likely to be some noticeable differences in your friend's behaviour, it may be more beneficial for them to see that your friendship hasn't changed. I'm not trying to say that you should pretend nothing is wrong, but try to act as you normally would around them and carry on doing things that you normally do together (i.e. going to the cinema).

# Opening up to my parents

One of the hardest things for me was telling my parents that I had an eating disorder, not because I didn't want to talk to them, but because I cared so much about them.

They had done so much for me from the day I was born, so how could I possibly tell them that I was starving myself? I didn't want to upset them or make them feel guilty for something that wasn't their fault. But I knew it had to be done.

I sat down in the living room with my mum and began to explain that I struggled with eating. At first, she thought this was purely a physical problem, but I then explained that it was something in my head telling me not to eat.

After our conversation, my parents did some research on eating disorders, which helped them to understand how I was feeling. From then onward, they have been so supportive and I couldn't thank them enough for being there for me. But these past few years haven't been easy for them either.

My eating disorder was turning me into someone I didn't want to be and I hated Anorexia for hurting my family and friends.

I remember a specific time when my parents were encouraging me to eat my meal. I wanted to do it, for them more than anything else, but I just couldn't. Instead, my frustration grew, and I ended up punching and kicking the door. Anyone who knows the real me would tell you that that's completely out of character, in fact my best friend didn't believe me when I first told her about it.

But times like this became more and more frequent and I can't begin to imagine how difficult it must have been for my parents to witness. But their support didn't just stop there.

During my admission, they would come to visit me and, when I was allowed supervised time away from the unit, they drove up just so I was able to go out. My mum often made the three hour train journey from home to the hospital, which I will forever be grateful for.

During the week, it was harder for my family to visit due to work commitments, but they never failed to keep in touch (via video message or text etc.).

# Interview: A mother's perspective

*An interview with my mum about how my eating disorders also affected her.*

<u>What is your favourite family moment?</u>
My favourite family moment is having Christmas Dinner at home with the family all together.

<u>How would you describe Anorexia Nervosa?</u>
I would describe it as an alien disease which takes over the mind and personality of the one you love.

<u>How did you feel when I was diagnosed?</u>
At the time, I was shocked and felt as if I was in a bubble with no way out. I was devastated and couldn't understand how this could have happened to my daughter.

<u>Did you think I could have got better without professional help?</u>
At the time, I didn't feel there was any way you were going to get better without professional help, although your Dad thought that the only way for you to recover was to be at home with the family. He felt as if he was letting you down, but in the end, it was inevitable that you received the help and care that you desperately needed.

<u>Was there ever a time when you thought my illness was untreatable?</u>
Yes. Every single day when I saw your bony body withering away into nothing, I was unable to see a light at the end of the tunnel. There were also quite a few specific times when I didn't think this illness was treatable. For example, the time when I caught you making an omelette with just the egg white or when I asked you to

have more bread one lunchtime and you replied with 'do I have to'. Seeing as you're now in a much better place, we sometimes laugh about these times, but back then, it was anything but funny.

How did you feel when I was admitted to hospital?
My thoughts were that it was our only hope for you to get better. And I think you also felt the same way. If you hadn't have been admitted when you were, you wouldn't have been here today, so the admission was a total Godsend.

What helped you to cope?
My faith really helped me to cope but the people from Church have just been absolutely amazing and so supportive throughout this difficult time in our lives. As well as this, being able to talk to my family and friends about how I feel was so important, because people don't tend to talk about your inner feelings, but it is so important.

Have you seen a change over the past year?
Yes I have definitely seen a change. You seem to have become a stronger and more assertive person and you now use your coping strategies that you have learnt from therapy. You're looking healthy again and your bubbly personality is flowing back

# Family Therapy

During my hospital admission, there was an option to receive family therapy if and when needed. For many families, it somehow carries a negative association, because they feel like it's trying to 'fix' something that isn't 'broken'. However, this is not how I viewed family therapy.

To me, it was a neutral environment where I could talk to my parents and discuss certain things. I was able to talk about things without anything getting even slightly heated and I also found out how my parents felt.

Family therapy was really insightful and I would certainly recommend it to others. Recovery from an eating disorder is much easier and more straightforward if the family get involved with their loved one's treatment too.

# My advice for parents

★ Be open with your children about your feelings, as it helps them to open up about theirs.

★ If you think your child might be suffering from an eating disorder, gently approach them at a time where you can properly talk and express your concerns in a calming manner.

★ Have a conversation with your child about what you can do to help them in their recovery.

★ Understandably, this is a difficult time for the whole family, but try not to get frustrated with your child. Let them know that it's not their fault and that you are there to support them.

★ Talking about body shape, weight or dieting can be quite triggering for someone with an eating disorder. Try to avoid conversations about these topics.

★ Although sometimes difficult to accept, nobody is immune from developing an eating disorder and therefore there is a potential for it to happen to your child too.

# Professionals

This section is aimed at people whose profession brings them into contact with eating disorder sufferers. Whether part of your everyday work, or only on occasion.

# Eating disorders in schools

For someone suffering from an eating disorder, school can be quite a daunting place. For me, it was somewhere where I put immense pressure on myself to get the highest grades possible, regardless of the impact on my own health and wellbeing.

Like many other people with Anorexia Nervosa, I would class myself as a perfectionist and to me, nothing was 'good enough' if it wasn't 100% or, in other words, 'perfect'. But the more obsessed I became with work, the less time I started spending with my friends. As time went on, I started to isolate myself more and more and 'swapped between friends' at lunchtime to avoid the daunting dining room.

I think it became obvious to many of my teachers that my health was deteriorating. But, even though some of the ones I was quite close to had asked me if everything was ok, Anorexia stopped me from telling them and told me I would be weak if I did. So instead, the words "I'm fine" just came out of my mouth, as if I was on autopilot. But the truth was, I wasn't fine. In fact, I was anything but fine.

To begin with, my eating disorder made me so determined to 'prove' that I was fine, that I purposefully ate 'normally' a couple of times in front of the teachers so that they would assume I was telling the truth.

I must say, that makes me sound very devious, which is very out of character for me and probably the reason why nobody thought twice about it. But anorexia turned me into someone I didn't recognise, and completely changed my personality.

**95**

# My advice for teachers

★ If you feel able to talk to a student who you suspect might have an eating disorder, make sure that you choose the right place and time to have a conversation. The best time would be when both you and the student have a sufficient amount of time to have a proper conversation, and not just a quick chat. I'd also recommend talking in a space that is fairly private, but also familiar to the student, as this may help them to feel more relaxed.

★ Of course, every situation is different, depending on the age of the student and perhaps the severity of their physical health. However, if someone does open up to you about struggling with an eating disorder, I think it is quite important to discuss the next steps with them and decide together what is going to happen next. For me, this would help me to not feel out of control, because I would be reassured that nothing would happen without me knowing about it.

★ It is important for the student to know that, above everything, their health is the priority. This may equate to them needing extensions for deadlines, or possibly someone to check in with them to find out how they're doing.

**96**

# GP's

GP's are often the first port of call for someone who thinks they may have an eating disorder, whether they have decided to go themselves or somebody has encouraged them to go.
Talking to a medical professional about their difficulties for the first time can be very daunting and it is important that the patient feels understood and listened to.

Although anorexia, bulimia and binge eating disorder are the 3 main eating disorders talked about in the media, OSFED (Other Specific Feeding and Eating Disorder), formerly EDNOS, is actually the most common eating disorder, although it is generally less well known.

Whilst some of my friends have had very positive experiences when visiting a GP to discuss their eating problems, many have found that their GP wasn't sure what to do or how to react, which left them waiting much longer for treatment than was necessary.
In some cases, patients have been told that they are "not ill enough" or that their weight "isn't critical yet".
But my argument would be that eating disorders are mental illnesses and, especially in the case of restrictive eating disorders, the patient can reach a point when their cognitive processing starts to slow down as a result of malnutrition. Therefore, the sooner a patient can get professional help (including therapy), the more likely they are to respond well to treatment.

# My advice for GP's

*GP's are often the first port of call for someone who is experiencing symptoms of an eating disorder. Here is a list of things that may be of help to GP's.*

★ Even if someone is experiencing symptoms of an eating disorder, but do not have a low weight or BMI, they still need to be taken seriously and given help as soon as possible.

★ Commenting on how a person looks can be quite triggering if they are suffering from an eating disorder.

★ Anorexia is not a part of a person's identity, so it might be useful to talk about the eating disorder as something separate from the sufferer.

★ To start with, I struggled to cope with weight gain. For me, the best solution was to be told whether my weight had gone up, down or stayed the same in a matter-of-fact way. It helped to not have a judgement attached, even if it was meant as a positive comment. For example, I would much rather be told 'your weight has gone up', than 'oh that's great, you're BMI has gone up by (X) amount, well done!' But seeing as other people may prefer a different approach, it's probably best to talk to the patient about what is most helpful for them.

★ If you are not sure how best to deal with the situation, the eating disorder charity Beat provides lots of information on their website, as well as through their helpline (also something that the patient can access).

# My experience of different therapies

*A piece I wrote for a talk to third year university students studying clinical psychology. It explores the different types of therapy I have received and which ones I found the most helpful.*

Hi,

My name is Rose Anne. I'm 20 and currently live in York, where I study French and German at the city's university. I love writing and playing music, fundraising for charity, playing squash and I'm always up for a good laugh. My friends would describe me as supportive, gentle, considerate and funny.

I've started off with my hobbies and values because that's who I truly am. That's the real me and the person I am when I'm well. At one point, my life was controlled by mental illness (and in particular my eating disorder). It felt like it was playing the lead role in my life, with the occasional appearance from Rose Anne whereas now, anorexia is in the background and I have resumed the lead role in my life.

For example, this time last year I was doing my A level exams and remember feeling such a strong and overwhelming sense of anxiety around food that the way I dealt with the situation was to avoid it altogether. This not only left me physically unwell, but also forced me to isolate myself from family and friends and miss out on social occasions and gatherings all because I was unable to cope with the food aspect.

**99**

One year on, radical acceptance has helped me to accept that, at least for now, I will still feel anxious around food and certain meals or types of food will make me feel more anxious than others. However, I also accept that my body needs fuel in order to survive and allow me to live a life that I value. I have realised that it is better to experience high levels of anxiety in the short term in order to have a better future in the long term.

As a quick background, I was diagnosed with Obsessive Compulsive Disorder as a teenager, for which I received cognitive behavioural therapy. As I began to manage my original intrusive thoughts and compulsions, the focus of these intrusions started to shift and my problems around food escalated, which led to a diagnosis of Anorexia Nervosa. In July 2015, I was admitted to an eating disorder inpatient unit, where I spent eight months receiving different types of therapy, such as Dialectic Behavioural Therapy and Acceptance and Commitment Therapy. After this, I started Day-patient treatment 2 days a week for eight hours each day. I then transferred to weekly outpatient treatment in York to prepare for moving to university.

Reducing the intensity of treatment was a very scary aspect for me, which is why I found Daycare to be so useful. From being on the unit, where all of your meals are pre-planned and made by the specialist chef to going home and then taking back the responsibility of catering for yourself is very difficult.

But Daycare meant that the step down in treatment wasn't as drastic. I attended twice a week, had breakfast, lunch and snacks with other patients, who subsequently became friends. With the help of the staff, we would choose meals which we found challenging and then afterwards, we would evaluate our levels of anxiety and how we felt both before, during and after the meal. Another helpful part of

**100**

Daycare was making a Wellness Recovery Action Plan (WRAP), which concentrates on exploring what you're like when you're well and what starts to change when you begin to struggle. It basically acts as a safety blanket, as it also explores triggers, coping strategies and encourages you to make a crisis plan in case you notice signs of relapse.

Having an experience of different types of therapy has enabled me to see what helps me and what isn't as helpful. Although CBT seemed useful at the time, I realise that it hasn't been as helpful as other types of therapy because, being a people-pleaser, I wanted to please my therapist and therefore tried to persuade myself that things were getting better each week.

Also, I now realise that the approach used for Radically Open Dialectic Behavioural Therapy is much more suited to me. This is because it helps you to find better ways to cope with difficult and stressful situations, rather than trying to change your way of thinking (something which is near impossible with someone who, like me, also has a diagnosis of autism).

I have found Radical Acceptance extremely useful, as it has helped me to be accepting of every situation I face and then find ways to adapt accordingly.

One way I have learnt to cope with stressful situations is to use Distress Tolerance, another helpful skill learnt from RODBT. This has helped me to calm myself down in anxiety-provoking circumstances and therefore enables me to think more positively and rationally.

The use of a self-soothe box helps with this. It contains items which cover all five of the senses and being mindful when using the box helps to make it even more effective.

I would say the main reason RODBT worked for me is because all of the skills seem to link together, allowing me to have a bigger 'toolbox' when faced with difficult situations.

I have also found Acceptance and Commitment Therapy to be a great help, as it focuses on my values and the things which are most important to me. I can then ask myself the underlying question 'Will my actions take me closer towards or further away from my values and being the person I want to be?'. This also allows me to listen to my own opinions and make my own choices rather than allowing anxiety to dictate my decisions and actions.

# Tips for clinicians

*Here are a few of my suggestions for therapists who are working with patients with an eating disorder.*

★ If a type of therapy doesn't seem to be helping, maybe try or suggest a different approach. It would also be helpful for you to tell the patient that different types of therapy work for different people and if something isn't working, it is not a reflection on them or the therapist.

★ Patience with the patient is key, as it often takes people a long time to open up and fully trust a therapist.

★ Get to know the patient a little:

- What are the patient's hobbies?

- What does the patient enjoy doing?

   (This allows you to develop a better relationship with the patient and helps them to see you as being 'on the same level' as them)

★ Talk about the positives:

- What is the patient doing well?

- What are their strengths?

- How can their strengths help them if they are struggling?

★ Although food, weight and body image are evidently part of eating disorders, they're very rarely the main issue. They're used as a coping mechanism for underlying struggles.

★ Everybody's story is different. Although a patient may have a diagnosis of an eating disorder, their behaviours, triggers and reasons behind developing an eating disorder will never be exactly the same as another person's.

★ Remember that many patients with an eating disorder will be more sensitive to certain comments concerning food/weight etc. so try to be careful with the things you say to them and how you say them.

**104**

# Tips for dieticians

*Having a dietician has been extremely helpful for me and has been a vital part of my recovery. Here are my five top tips for dieticians working with eating disorder patients.*

1. **Arrange regular meetings**

   I found it reassuring to have regular meetings with my dietician and it enabled me to regularly discuss things I found difficult throughout the week as well as talk about what challenges I would set for the following week.

   During my admission, our meetings with the dietician would mostly be when our meal plans were being increased, which made them quite stressful and anxiety provoking.

2. **Be approachable**

   It helps if a dietician is cheerful and friendly during sessions, as this makes them less anxiety-provoking. Developing a good relationship is important, so the patient can see that you are on their side. If you feel it's appropriate, don't be afraid to have a laugh and a joke with the patient, as this helps to make the atmosphere more relaxed.

3. **Treat each case individually**

   Having a meal plan that was adapted for me has made meals a lot more manageable. As I have a diagnosis of High Functioning Autism, I often find that my senses can be heightened in certain atmospheres. Specific textures, such as 'smooth' foods are intolerable for me when I am anxious and finding a solution to this with my dietician has made it much easier to deal with. Because eating disorders can present in so many different ways, I found it extremely helpful when my dietician discussed my personal difficulties and then helped me to find ways to challenge those difficulties.

4. **Discuss nutrition education**

Nutrition education has played a huge role in challenging my eating disorder because it helps to rationalise my thoughts. Even some of the most logical things are distorted by Anorexia. For example, to most people it is obvious that the more activity you do in a day, the more fuel your body needs to function, but this wasn't important in Anorexia's eyes and so this, along with other common sense facts, were totally disregarded. I also talked to my dietician about portion sizes, which made me realise that this was where I was possibly slipping. I found it useful to take pictures of my meals and then I sometimes went through these in my next session. Specifically for me, we were able to see that at times when my portion sizes weren't sufficient, I would either not take a picture of the meal or, more frequently, I would look at the picture afterwards, realise the portion was small and then not show that picture to my dietician. This helped immensely, as, at times when I didn't want to show the picture, I was able to stop, take a step back and reflect why this was the case.

5. **Make the meal plan simple**

Whilst I was an inpatient, every snack was given a letter depending on its nutritional value. Whilst at the time, I found this comforting, I later realised that it was very hard to adjust into 'normal eating'. Every element of the meal was specifically calculated. A bagel was seen as more substantial than two slices of bread and therefore, instead of having an 'F' for dessert ( a Yorkie for example), I would have an 'E' (a Dairy Milk). In a way, this lettering system just reinforced my belief that every single calorie mattered. If our snack was an 'A' fruit, we were only allowed an apple or an orange, but

**106**

not a banana, because that was classed as a 'B'. It has taken me a long time to 'relearn' that a chocolate bar is a chocolate bar and a piece of fruit includes both apples and bananas, but it was worth it because I no longer worry about what 'letter label' is given to a certain food. Instead, I am able to choose what I want to eat and not what is 'right for the plan'.

# Useful aids

My Personal food hierarchy

For me, visual aids are really useful, as they are more appealing and I am therefore more likely to use them. This is my own version of a food hierarchy. Since different foods change position very regularly, I like to be able to move the pictures around so that I can keep my hierarchy up to date. This picture was taken a while ago and I'm happy to say that many for foods are now nearer to the green end of the chart. Knowing this helps me to see how much progress I have made, because it is often difficult for me to see the positive changes and steps towards recovery .

# Eating Disorder research at the University of York

*Contributed my PhD student Mark Carey*

I'm a second year Psychology PhD student at the University of York, and I've been kindly allowed to share some of the research that I am doing in the department. My work focuses on body perception and emotions in relation to clinical eating disorders, and eating disorder vulnerability within the non-clinical population.

A common symptom found within eating disorders is a strong dissatisfaction towards one's own body, and this remains a key target for therapy. It has been reported that many current therapies such as cognitive-behavioural therapy focus largely on the emotional component of the disorder, providing coping strategies and techniques for patients to combat any intrusive negative thoughts relating to their body image. However, growing research suggests that body dissatisfaction may be influenced by an inaccurate perceptual experience of the body, and this is largely overlooked within treatment. It is argued that the 'feeling of fatness' that is often reported amongst patients may be from a misperception of one's actual body size, rather than simply persistent negative thinking. It is thought that treatments which target and improve this inaccurate perceptual experience could protect against relapses of the disorder.

Research conducted in our department by Dr. Catherine Preston found that changes in the perceived size of one's own body directly influenced feelings of body dissatisfaction amongst healthy individuals. This was achieved using an illusion experiment, such that individuals felt ownership over an obese body as though it was their own. To put this another way, when the individual felt like they owned a larger body, they felt more dissatisfied with their body. This direct link has been shown both behaviourally and in the brain activity of the individuals, as brain areas associated with body perception and emotion processing showed increased activation during this experiment.

These links between body perception and body satisfaction may help us understand why relapse is so high within clinical eating disorders. An inaccurate experience of your own body can understandably trigger negative emotions. Without improvement in this experience, it may leave an individual vulnerable to relapse if the coping strategies acquired in therapy break down. Our research aims to further investigate this perceptual aspect of the disorder, using multisensory body illusions and augmented reality techniques. More information regarding eating disorders can be found via the Beat charity website: https://www.b-eat.co.uk/.

# Bird Flying Free

Here are some of the posts from my blog http://roseanneevans.com
If you would like to read more like this, feel free to visit my
website, or like my Facebook page Bird Flying Free.

# Be a friend to yourself

In a recent therapy session, I was asked to sketch a person and around it, write the things I believe make a good friend.
Some of the things I wrote included being kind and caring, treating others with respect, occasionally treating your friend, being understanding and patient ... the list goes on. I was then told to imagine that this friend was, in fact, myself and was asked whether I treated myself the same way that I would treat all of my other friends. I hesitantly replied with a simple 'no'.

My therapist asked me what differences there were to the way I treated myself in comparison to others. I said that I wasn't kind to myself, I didn't take care of myself, I hardly ever treated myself and I definitely was not understanding or patient with myself! Suddenly, the penny dropped.

How could I expect others to treat me nicely if I was being an awful friend to myself? Surely that was just hypocritical?

To me, the first step is realising that you need to be your own friend and look after yourself, but then the harder part is actually putting that into practice.

It often helps me to spend a few minutes in each situation thinking about how I would treat my friends if they were in my position, or what they would do to make me feel better if they were with me. This is because my reactions to certain situations have become ingrained and habitual, which means it takes me a bit longer than usual to think both rationally and compassionately.

Like anything that has become a habit, it takes time to change your ways and my advice would be to build up being compassionate to yourself.

To start with, treat yourself to a new nail varnish or go for a massage. Allow yourself food that you want and enjoy, no matter what your eating disorder is telling you. To start with, try to do one extra thing every day to take extra care of yourself and then increase this to twice a day.

If, like me, you find it difficult to relax and feel guilty for not constantly doing something productive, maybe try to compromise. After every hour (for example) you spend doing something productive, allow yourself to have a break for a certain length of time (I'd recommend at least half an hour). A relaxing activity could be anything from watching one of your favourite films, to reading an enjoyable (and preferably fictional) book. Doing this allows you to find the balance between 'work' and 'play', which hopefully will enable you to de-stress.

The main thing I took from this therapy session was that I need to be kind and treat both myself and my body well. It has taught me to be my own friend as, that way, there will always be someone there looking after me.

For me, a major hurdle when learning to be kind to myself was that I would often get frustrated and 'beat myself up' in my head. At times when my eating disordered thoughts were more powerful, I would tell myself that I was 'being stupid' and that I 'am pathetic'. To be honest, the way I speak to myself when these conflicts occur is quite shocking and I would certainly never say the same things to my friends. I have come to realise that the best way to fight against that voice in your head telling you not to eat is to focus on being gentle with yourself. Think about what you would say to a friend experiencing the same level of distress. For me, that means telling myself in a caring and calm manner that I know things are difficult and I know it isn't easy. I reassure myself that everything will be ok and that doing the opposite of what anorexia is telling me to do will help me to move closer towards my goal of living a normal, healthy and happy life.

I hope this also helps you to realise that being kind to yourself is very important, and that it is OK to put yourself before others!! This does not mean you are selfish or inconsiderate, it just means that you are tending to your own needs (a vital part of recovery).

So please be kind to yourself. Give yourself time to relax and enjoy life. You are the best person to give yourself the TLC which you truly deserve!

Onwards and upwards,

R.A.E xx

# Reaching recovery goals

This week, I have reached a milestone in my recovery by being discharged from Daycare at the hospital where I also received inpatient treatment. This got me thinking about how it feels when you reach different points or goals in recovery.

The way I like to see it is there are two different points of view. Firstly, there is the eating disorder. It makes me feel guilty every time I move a step closer towards recovery. It tells me that recovery isn't going to make me happier, but following its rules will. It makes me have negative feelings towards recovery, I feel like I am no longer ill enough and sometimes it tells me that I never was ill.

But now I am able to listen to my rational mind. Now I actually listen to me and not Anorexia.

Deep down I know that my eating disorder will not make me happier and being thinner will not solve any of my problems. Although my eating disorder sometimes tries to distort my memories and make me think I was happier when I was at a low weight, I know that this is not the case.

In fact, it was quite the opposite!! Every day was a struggle: even getting out of bed was a chore, I was completely exhausted all of the time and I was constantly cold. I isolated myself from family and friends and wasn't really living the life I had imagined.

But now, I am able to go out and not feel completely out of energy when I get home. I can play squash when I want to and because I enjoy it, not because my eating disorder forces me to. After a long

**115**

wait, I can finally go on holiday with my best friend and her family and enjoy it without constantly worrying about food or wearing a bikini on the beach. And after having to defer my place at university last year, I can gladly say I am well enough to go to uni in September to study French and German!

So no matter how much your eating disorder tries to tell you that you will be happier if you follow its rules, please trust that it is not telling you the truth. Maybe try to write down everything you have done or achieved whilst you are well so at times when you're struggling, you can look back and see how much better your life in recovery is compared to when you were in the depths of an eating disorder.

Reaching goals in recovery is such a positive thing and you should be proud of yourself for battling on. So keep going, live the life YOU want to and don't sacrifice it just to please your eating disorder.

Onwards and upwards,

R.A.E xx

# Music in recovery

One major part of my recovery has been music. Not only does listening to music help to calm me down and explain how I am feeling, but actually playing an instrument acts as a great source of therapy for me. I have played the clarinet for many years and have found it to be an aid to help me express my emotions (something which I otherwise find incredibly difficult).Over the past year, I have started singer/song writing and this has proven to be an invaluable hobby in terms of recovery.

I started by writing poetry, as using rhyme allowed me to verbalise my inner feelings, because even I wasn't consciously aware of how I felt. One day, I decided to add some guitar chords to one of my poems, as this helps to show what mood I was in when writing the poem.

Since that day, I have written over twenty songs and enjoy playing them in front of family and friends. I hope that someday I will build up enough confidence to be able to play these songs in public, however the key thing at present is that I am able to use song writing as a way to let out my emotions and express them in a healthier and more controlled way.

Because I want to help others suffering from mental illness, many of my songs include positive messages about getting through difficult times and even if my music only helps one person, I will be so happy!!

So if you're looking for something to help you in recovery, creative activities such as music or art are great ways to express yourself!!

Even if you don't feel like trying it because maybe you'll 'make a fool of yourself', or you're 'not good at anything', give it a go! After all, you'll never know for certain until you give things a go!

Onwards and upwards,

R.A.E Xx

# POETRY

At times when I struggle to explain how I am feeling, I turn to poetry and song-writing as a means of expressing myself. These poems are all written for different reasons, such as for explaining how Anorexia makes you feel or for encouraging myself and others to keep on fighting.

# A life without Ana

When you feel all alone
And you've lost all your hope
A friend comes along
And she helps you to cope.

But this friend isn't good,
She pretends to be nice
You listen to her
And take on her advice.

But she's evil, this friend
And she takes all control
She takes hold of your life
And takes hold of your soul.

But you still take on board
All the things that she says
You think she is right
And you follow her ways.

But this evil friend
Has just one goal in sight
She wants you to fail
And give up the fight.

You then start to realise
That she's not your friend
The one thing she wants
Is for your life to end

Then you go against her
And show her who's boss
But she has an answer
For all bridges you cross

I know it may seem
That she is the best way
To make all your troubles
And fears go away

But you are much stronger
Than you like to think
Just trust in yourself
Because you will not sink

Now look to the future
And you will soon see
A life without Ana,
Your arch enemy.

# My journey to recovery

My journey to recovery
will not be a smooth ride.
But I know I will get there soon,
I can feel it inside.

I know that I need to stay strong
And let my thoughts pass by.
The less I let them bother me,
the more those thoughts will die.


These thoughts that I get in my head
Fill me with utter fear.
But the less I react to them,
The less they will appear.

So now I know what I must do,
Determined I will stay.
This illness will not defeat me,
I will be free one day

**121**

# So called friend

My journey began
With a so called friend
Who said if I lost weight
All my worries would end.

She stopped me from eating
She stole all my pride
I felt so much fear
I just wanted to hide.

She says you'll be happy
With your next target weight
But all you receive
Is a dark, gloomy fate.

You know that she's lying
You know that she's wrong,
But you're stuck in this cycle
That's hard to break from.

I want to be normal
I want to be free
From this so called friend
Who's got a grip on me.

# I am a bird

I am a bird
I've been set free
Trapped in a cage
Is where I used to be

I am a bird
I'm flying high
I spread my wings
And soar into the sky

I see the world in a new light
The land is green and the sea is blue
And I look back and see where I've come from

**123**

The clouds were grey and the rain falls too.
I was lost
But I've been found
My head was buried
Underneath the ground

I was lost
But I've found my way
And now I cherish
Every single day

There's such beauty on this earth
Never forget how much your life is worth
There isn't anything you can't mend
For every fairy tale has a happy end

I am strong
But I once was weak
The world around me
Seemed so dark and bleak

I am strong
And I'll stand up tall
To all my demons
I will fight them  all

**124**

# Make a wish upon a star

To my dear friend, you'll be ok.
Believe, and you will find your way.
As difficult as your life seems,
You can and will fulfil your dreams.

I know right now, it's hard to find
A way to leave your past behind,
To live your life and not give in
To thoughts and feelings deep within.

Remember that you have the choice
To listen to  your inner voice.
You know just what you want and need
So that in life, you can succeed

I cannot say that this will be
A struggle-free recovery.
But sometimes in the darkest night,
The stars appear so clear and bright.

So make a wish upon a star
That you will see how loved you are.
Oh please don't let this be the end,
My beautiful and worthy friend.

**125**

# Fighter

I'm going to get through this,
to me that is clear.
I'll get to the point
Where my thoughts cause no fear.

I am a fighter,
I'll never give in,
I'll fight with this illness,
And I know I'll win.

It will be exhausting
And it will take time
But this mental illness
Is no friend of mine.

I'll no longer allow it
To take hold of me.
It will lose all control
And soon I will be free.

To let my thoughts go
Is my ultimate aim.
They'll pass through my mind
And they'll cause me no pain.

I'll carry on smiling,
As I always do.
It's not always easy,
But I'll battle through.

**126**

So if you are struggling,
Please open your eyes.
You're braver and stronger
Than you realise.

**127**

# I want to be free

There's no easy way
To get rid of these voices
Which control my thoughts
And change all my own choices.

I want to be normal.
I want to be free
From these awful voices
Which take hold of me.

It's one constant battle
in my single mind.
There's Demon, he's evil
And Angel is kind.

The angel is peaceful,
Though she's not as strong.
But she'll fight with the Demon
If something is wrong.

The Demon is louder,
He's always around.
Just one single mouthful
And he'll make a sound.

He'll tell me I'm worthless,
He'll tell me I'm weak,
That I am a nothing
And I am a freak.

**128**

So then I obey him
And do what he says.
I've been stuck in this cycle
For too many days.

He's changed me completely,
I'm no longer myself.
I've forsaken my friendships,
My life and my health.

# The dream I've longed to chase

As I sit and listen to the sound
of sweet birds singing all around
the wind, oh so gentle, touches my face
this is the dream I've longed to chase.

The water gently flows along
and I'm so sure this is where I belong
My mind is so silent, peaceful and calm
It is stunned by the beauty of nature's pure charm.

I've always longed to feel this way,
And now I am certain it's where I must say.
I am determined to get back on track,
And I won't let anything hold me back.

My future looks bright and I'm hopeful to see
The life that is patiently waiting for me.
I'll fight all anxiety, fear and doubt
So that I can beat this and find a way out.

# <u>Thank You</u>

I would just like to say a big thank you to everyone who has helped to make this book a reality.
Without your support, it wouldn't have been possible and so I'm eternally grateful to you all!

I hope this book has helped you to understand more about Anorexia Nervosa regardless of how much or little you previously knew.

Writing this book has also been very rewarding and therapeutic for me, as it has enabled me to see the reasons behind my struggle. I believe I was given this challenge in order to help and inspire other people out there.

Onwards and upwards,

Rose Anne Evans!

Printed in Great
Britain
by Amazon